# Crying, Learning and Laughing:

*Why Students Visit the Teen Center*

## Tamika M. Murray

*Celestial Publishing, LLC*

ISBN: 978-1-7350293-0-6

Cover design by OliviaProDesign on Fiverr.com.

Edited by Casanova Green on Fiverr.com

Formatted by Accuracy4Sure on Fiverr.com

Printed in Vineland, New Jersey

Published by Celestial Publishing, LLC

CelestialPublishingllc.com

MikaMurray.com


Publisher's Cataloging-in-Publication Data
provided by Five Rainbows Cataloging Services

Names: Murray, Tamika M., author.

Title: Crying, learning, and laughing : why students visit the teen center / Tamika M. Murray.

Description: Vineland, NJ : Celestial Publishing, 2020. | Includes bibliographical references.

Identifiers: LCCN 2020912414 (print) | ISBN 978-1-73502-930-6 (paperback) | ISBN 978-1-73502-931-3 (ebook)

Subjects: LCSH: School social work. | Teenagers--Mental health. | Students--Mental health services. | School health services. | BISAC: SOCIAL SCIENCE / Social Work.

Classification: LCC LB3013.4 .M87 2020 (print) | LCC LB3013.4 (ebook) | DDC 371.4/6--dc23.

# Contents

**PART IV**

**PART V**

**PART VI**

**PART VII**

# Dedication

This book is dedicated to my mother (R.I.P.), who helped me develop a love of reading and writing, to Darcy for proofreading my drafts, to Ramon for supporting my dreams, and the Teen Center students and staff because there wouldn't be a book without you.

# Pay It Forward

Thank you for setting aside time to read my book. After you finish reading, please feel free to do the optional acts suggested below.

Leave a review on
www.Amazon.com and/or www.Goodreads.com.

Share a post about this book on social media.

Tell at least three people about the book.

Follow me on social media
https://www.instagram.com/celestialscribe81/
https://www.instagram.com/celestialpublishingllc/
https://www.facebook.com/TheCelestialScribe

Email me @MikaMurray81@gmail.com if you'd like to discuss a writing project or the issues discussed in the book.

## Part I

# Overview of School-Based

# Youth Services Programs

# Introduction

————◆◆◇◆◇————

The struggle is real for adolescents facing peer pressure, crime-riddled streets, intimate relationships, chaotic homes, absentee parents, and more. My job as a Family Service Specialist brought me into the dysfunctional lives of teens in need of education, guidance, and nurturing. But requesting a check for utilities, rent, or clothing isn't the way I wanted to help our youth.

As an experienced Adjunct English Instructor, my conversations with previous students and current clients grew lengthy as we discussed everyday life. I often found it difficult to conduct short home visits because our talks trailed off into school, life goals, hobbies, places to visit, and job hunting tips.

A few years after leaving the Division of Child Protection and Permanency (D.C.P.P.), a job ad on Indeed.com grabbed my attention. The extensive duties and requirements didn't dissuade me because I love a good challenge. After playing phone tag with an HR representative, my first interview got scheduled. It went well and led to a second interview. This time I presented a PowerPoint slide show on handling a teen break up. Then the observation and interaction with the students occurred.

My tightened chest didn't stop me from awkwardly engaging with teens, unsure of my abilities. But I must have done something right because the journey of crying, learning, and laughing with the Teen Center kids began.

The stories, tips, and information explored in this book took two academic years to gather. From my first day of work playing card games and watching *Fuller House* to greeting struggling teens like Lil Purple, the goal of resolving crises and answering questions took precedence. So sit back, get comfortable, and learn why students visit the Teen Center.

# Chapter One

# How Do School-Based Youth Services Work?

————◆————

**W**aking up at 6:00 AM never came easy for me. I loathed the process as a student and resented it as an employee. But if you agree to abide by a company's rules, then sucking it up becomes the norm. Living with an underactive thyroid didn't help my body's craving for sleeping in late.

I'd roll out of bed and move with the pace of a sleep-deprived zombie. Performing the morning ritual of selecting an outfit required too much effort, so I did it the night before.

After the usual bathroom activities, my three kitties needed their breakfast. I also made sure the trapped, spayed, and neutered feral kitties got some sustenance too.

On a good day, my skinny butt was out the door by 7:00. But if my slow energy couldn't push me forward, 7:15 sparked a rushed commute.

The comedic stylings of the *Tom Joyner Morning Show* gave me life through Shaun King news, R&B music, and Chris Paul and Huggy Lowdown humor.

Many days I arrived with just enough time to turn on the computers, unlock the cabinets, sign into the necessary portals, and review my schedule before that first knock on the door at 7:54-ish.

On a quiet day, the mental health clinician, part-time case manager, intern, and I could speak with the students while listening to music or playing Uno. If the Universe was cranky, endless tears and loud talking teens in need of a private chat greeted us.

Life at the Teen Center followed the school's periods, but no two days ran the same. If your school, city, or state doesn't offer an in-school program of this kind, then your kids are missing out.

## What Is a Teen Center?

In New Jersey, the School-Based Youth Services Program (SBYSP) or Teen Centers receive funding by the New Jersey Department of Children and Families' (DCF) Division of Family and Community Partnerships (FCP), Office of School Linked Services (OSLS). The department allocates the funds to an agency or organization of their choice to set up the school-based services within an elementary, middle school, or high school. While each Teen Center offers similar services, our school's center provided:

- College, job, and scholarship application assistance
- Girls, Boys, Mental Health, and Pregnancy Prevention Groups
- Guest speakers
- Individual counseling
- Leadership recognition
- Referrals to community services
- Trips (college tours, conferences, and recreation)
- Tutoring

- Volunteer opportunities

Returning students loved getting a pass for lunch or study hall, which lasted until June unless they earned poor grades, had excessive absences, or cut class too often. Freshman learned of the Teen Center through orientation, upper classmen, classroom presentations, or our freshman summer program. But, the Teen Center was more than a place to eat lunch or get a snack.

## Hours of Operation

Our doors were open Monday through Friday from 7:30 AM to 3:30 PM, twelve months a year, unless otherwise stated. An observable holiday, event, field trip, and inclement weather might alter the Teen Center hours.

## Parental Consent

Teen Center policy required a signed Social Services Rights and Consent form from a student's parent or guardian after one visit. Students 18 years or older could sign the form, but tracking down students to get signed consent forms was easier said than done.

If a student needed clinical services, the mental health clinician distributed the therapist's packet. Scheduling an intake appointment happened after the return of the completed forms.

## Extra Support

Adolescence is stressful no matter what neighborhood you're from, what school you attend, and what your parents do for a living. Yet, a teen's home and community profoundly impact their life. Students struggling to buy new clothes, attend prom, or find a job turned to us.

We distributed donated clothing and prom tickets and took the time to help them search for gigs hiring 15 and 16-year-olds. If they couldn't understand an assignment, we attempted to explain the directions. If it was math-related, my help was limited.

## A Safe Place

What students disclosed to us remained confidential unless it involved suicide, abuse, neglect, or threats to harm someone else. Even when students trusted a colleague or me with sensitive information, it remained with the necessary staff.

The day my first student admitted to suicidal thoughts within the past week, my anxiety went through the roof. Of course, we received training to handle those types of situations. But when it's happening, your mind can go blank.

I sat there asking the proper questions, and once I had confirmation of those thoughts, I sought my program director whose office was across from mine. Her chair was empty. In hindsight, I should have asked our mental health clinician for help, but I'd become so accustomed to asking my boss that asking anyone else seemed "wrong."
But I'd left the student with our mental health clinician and searched for my boss in the school to no avail.

Moments later, she returned and helped me take the next steps. To get information about suicide, child abuse, or bullying prevention into the right hands, we used table events and presentations. Brochures, pamphlets, and giveaways lined our table in the cafeteria as curious lunchtime munchers asked what we were doing. To satisfy job requirements, we made the rounds to various classes to discuss teen dating violence and bullying always letting the kids know we were available to talk.

## Someone to Listen

It may seem like common sense that a Teen Center offered individual counseling, but you'd be surprised at the number of students unaware of that service. No matter how many kids flocked to us, new ones found their way each month. We did plenty of outreach, but referrals from the guidance counselors and teachers streamlined the process.

One day as my lunch break began in the common area, a student came in to talk. I apologized for eating at the table, but the teen didn't mind because the floodgates of a first love break-up ran down a sallow face. The ending of a relationship is never easy, so for an adolescent to trust a stranger in an open area speaks volumes. I offered a second session once my shared office was free, but the student already began to feel better.

On a different day, another student accompanied by a close friend disclosed information that resulted in the Division of Protection and Permanency conducting an investigation. The student remained in the home but enjoyed speaking with me about the impact of the disclosure on the grandparents and other personal issues.

But having someone to listen to your troubles could mean the difference between life and death if the teen's depression is untreated. Therefore, giving students access to resources makes a positive difference.

## Access to Resources

A trip to the Teen Center could result in acquiring art supplies for a project, details about an upcoming field trip, or holiday presents. The free individual counseling services and groups tackling pregnancy prevention gave the pupils quality mental health and social service care.

Our connections with local organizations and yearly grant funding allowed kids to receive what they needed to finish assignments, attend educational conferences, and hear lectures from local program representatives. The inspirational guest speakers encouraged many of the teens to become active members of the community, thereby sparking an interest in volunteering in the Teen Center or the food bank. The Stand-Up and Rebel group, facilitated by a local non-profit, empowered our kids to ignore peer pressure to use drugs, alcohol, and tobacco products.

## Leadership Recognition

Some teens step into leadership positions more quickly than others. As a token of our appreciation for volunteering, the Teen Center honored a student each month. Student selection occurred through ballots and discussions of the Teen Center staff. The winner received a certificate, movie ticket, popcorn, and candy inside a popcorn holder. We posted their picture with a blurb on the bulletin board next to the front door.

The kids waited anxiously every month for the big lunchtime reveal. However, we couldn't please everyone. For example, one time, when a student's identity was revealed, her close friend grabbed her own wig, twirled it, tossed it and playfully chased, and laughter ensued. It was just another memorable day at the Teen Center.

## Discussion Questions

1. Do you think Teen Centers are useful?

2. Would you recommend a teen to utilize their services?

3. Why do you think Teen Centers are necessary?

# Part II

# Social Service Issues

# Chapter Two

# How Do You Prevent and Handle Teen Dating Violence?

---

E ach school day, students hold hands and kiss against lockers, longing for classes to end. They ignore the cacophony of hallway sounds while smiling ear to ear. Straining eyes and tiring fingers by texting until midnight.

The relationship progresses to couple selfies, canceling on friends, covering up bruises, loss of appetite, and crying oneself to sleep, making excuses for why the anger started. Wishing things would go back to the beginning. Wanting to leave, but don't know how?

## What Is Teen Dating Violence?

Teen dating violence or "intimate relationship violence among adolescents" involves harassment, stalking, physical, psychological, or sexual abuse of a person 12 to 18 years old in a romantic relationship (1).

## How Was It Handled in the Teen Center?

While teen dating violence sounds easy to recognize for adults, teens are often unaware of the signs and what to do to get out of the situation. During my time as a Teen Center case manager, we encountered students concerned for their friends, siblings, or themselves. They were sometimes secretive and nervous about disclosing information.

But when guest speakers, films, or bulletin boards provided helpful real-life stories and resources, this opened the door to discussions. Several of the kids on my caseload thanked me for taking the time to review what a healthy relationship includes.

## Student Zero

"Do you think about the type of man you want to marry or raise your kids?"

"No. I never thought about it," Student Zero shrugged.

'Well, since you're doing adults things with your boyfriend, it's time to start thinking about adult consequences."

"True," said Student Zero while looking down.

"Sure, you won't be getting married soon. But if an unexpected pregnancy happens, then things change. Will your boyfriend be able to support you? Does he want children some day?"

"We don't talk about it. But I'm glad you talk about this stuff."

"Now is the time you're developing relationship skills. Whatever you're willing to put up with might carry over into adulthood. If you accept cheating, name calling, hitting, fighting, or other nonsense now, the pattern could continue into other relationships. Besides, being with someone doesn't mean one person gets to be happy.

**17**

Partnerships should be 50/50."

"I never thought about it." "That's okay. It's why I'm here."
When I asked students if their parents ever spoke with them about relationships and what they should look like, too many said, "No, my parents never talk with me unless I'm in trouble."

As February grew closer, preparations for the activities, bulletin board, and table events began. Sometimes, I'd conduct random bulletin board searches while watching something on TV at home. Or a memory of a conversation with a past D.C.P.P. client might remind me of what to say to the adolescents to prevent an unhealthy partnership. The dialogue for teen dating violence started at the beginning of the year as the part-time case manager, andI made our rounds to the freshman health classes. Our presentation consisted of a PowerPoint slide show and the short film, *Aleah*.

The film presents an all too familiar character living in a drug and gun infested neighborhood. Aleah's home life is lonely since her un-nurturing mother works long hours and provides hurtful blows when learning of Aleah's dilemma.

Some students from the freshman summer program saw the 1996 made-for-TV-movie, *No One Would Tell*, starring Fred Savage and Candace Cameron Bure. It was based on the true story of a fatal teen dating violence relationship.

To bring the subject into the Teen Center, the use of the large bulletin board highlighted real accounts of girls killed by abusive boyfriends, which got many of the regulars to take notice. Plus, the guest speakers from the local women's center added to the conversation by addressing the signs of teen dating violence and steps to get help. Putting a face to an organization designed to help women and children made the resources feel more accessible.

## Prevention is Essential

When it comes to teen dating violence, prevention is the key to saving lives. To keep your son or daughter safe from an unhealthy and potentially harmful relationship, you should know what to look for before it happens. Ensure you know the signs of an abusive, intimate relationship.

Below is a list of information for you and your teen to determine if their relationship is an example of teen dating violence:

- Partner constantly criticizes you
- Controls your clothing, activities, behavior
- Coercion or pressure to become sexual
- Ignores your pleas to stop hugging, kissing, touching, and other sexual behaviors
- Refuses to use a condom or forces you to take birth control
- Limits your time with friends, family, or co-workers
- Has a bad temper or becomes jealous easily
- Excessively texts or calls you
- Stops by your home unexpectedly
- Bites, hits, punches, shoves, slaps, or spits on you
- Wants to get committed too fast
- Blames you when he/she treats you badly
- Uses your passwords to monitor texts and social media

While this list isn't comprehensive, it's the right combination of the types of behavior found in an abusive relationship.

After discussing the signs, take action. Talk with your son or daughter if you suspect the relationship is unhealthy. Inform him or her of the signs of a teen dating violence partnership. If your teen is single, get them familiar with this information. Let them know you're there to help.

Seek counseling if you think it's necessary. Provide the phone number to a local women's shelter or the National Teen Dating Abuse Hotline phone number 1-866-331-9474 (2). If they are in immediate danger, tell them to callthe police.

When he or she does date, please get to know their boyfriend or girlfriend. Use your intuition to guide you. If something feels off, please don't ignore it. Make your kids aware of what a healthy, functional relationship should look like through leading by example.

Children learn in their environment, so what is said and done within the home impacts their lives. Many teens fall into an abusive relationship because they saw it at home. But, you can help break the cycle.

## The Consequences

"Violent behavior often begins between 6th and 12th grade (3)." Even more alarming is about 1.5 million American high school students disclosed they were "physically harmed or intentionally hit" by a romantic partner. The relationships experienced during adolescence can set the tone for future partnerships.

Taking the time to sit down, listen, and talk with a teen can bring surprising results. Not only will it let them know you're supportive, but they will also have someone to vent their emotions. Teens without a secure connection to a parent or caregiver might turn to whoever gives them attention. This type of behavior makes them vulnerable to attracting the wrong people.

If teen dating violence is left untreated, it could lead to pregnancy, contraction of a sexually transmitted disease or infection, anxiety, depression, substance abuse, use of tobacco products, bullying, lying, hospitalization, suicide attempts, or death.

## Take Action Now

Not all high school students have a Teen Center in high school. Parents, teachers, guidance counselors, school social workers, and mentors need to educate teens about relationships. If you believe an adolescent is in a dangerous situation, please intervene or tell someone who can.

## Discussion Questions

1. Did you ever witness teen dating violence when you were an adolescent?

2. Have you ever been in an abusive relationship?

3. Do you believe teen dating violence is preventable? Why? Why not?

# Chapter Three

# How Do You Protect Your Teens from STDs?

———◆◇◆———

**H**ot-blooded teens caught up in the moment aren't thinking about Gonorrhea, Chlamydia, or Herpes. What transpires in a matter of minutes might lead to a lifetime consequence. So, parents, guardians, social workers, and teachers need to educate pre-teens and teens before it's too late.

## What Are STDs/STIs?

Sexually transmitted diseases or infections are contracted through intimate contact, sexual activity, and exchange of bodily fluids such as blood, saliva, and semen. Although research provides the necessary knowledge to prevent these diseases, a stigma continues to surround them. HIV and AIDS have been around since the early 1980s, but people still fear contracting it from interactions with HIV-positive people.

Before working at the teen center, I worked in a resource home for gay and bisexual males with HIV or AIDS. Listening to heartbreaking stories of them being tossed away by family and society was depressing, yet informative. It triggered a memory of a previous student.

During my time as an Adjunct English Instructor, a quiet student revealed her HIV status in an essay. The truth knocked me over since we were both African American women in our mid-twenties.

By my arrival at the Teen Center, I gained valuable experience from dealing with adolescents and adults living with the consequences of poor decisions and risky behavior.

## Four Ways STDs Were Handled in the Teen Center

Life in the Teen Center was never dull. But whenever a lull appeared, we knew it was merely the calm before another storm. No one wants to imagine a child or adolescent contracting an STD. Unfortunately, acquiring an STD is a reality for many individuals, not just adults.

Every year, people ages 15-24 contract half of the 20 million new cases. Even more alarming is two in five sexually active females have infertility causing STDs, and "80 percent of HIV diagnoses" among adolescents ages, 13 to 19 are male.

While many parents want to focus on pregnancy prevention, it's vital to speak with your teens about safe sex. Yes, abstinence is the best way to protect your son or daughter against an STD; however, not all adolescents will wait until marriage or a long-term relationship. By giving them exposure to information and resources, you're empowering them.

## The Bulletin Board

To celebrate STD awareness month in April, a bulletin board in the Teen Center incorporated Pokémon with the theme of STD prevention. The title "Don't Catch Em All" sparked interest and curiosity about the different types of STDs. Through using a well-known cartoon, the Teen Center regulars grew interested in a topic that sometimes makes them look the other way. But once their attention was captured, I did show them pictures of external symptoms and reviewed the health issues involved.

## Table Events

Setting up a table in the cafeteria attracted the usual crowd and newcomers, too. The spinning wheel, trivia questions, pamphlets, brochures, and prizes allowed the dialogue to flow. Many of the teens spoke with us towards the end of their lunch; some stayed to find out more.

## Teen Conference

The Planned Parenthood Annual Teen Conference gave the Teen Center and its attendees the chance to have funwhile learning. Th e trip to Rowan University for the conference allowed the kids to see a college campus and look toward the future.

Safe sex, self-image, surviving abuse, pregnancy prevention, LGBTQ+, bullying, suicide, leadership, drug prevention and many other topics were covered through interactive shows, workshops, and activities. There were multiple organizations present to distribute handouts, pens, and other valuable items.

## One-on-One Sessions

When it came to discussing STD prevention with students, it could be eye-opening. Many of the kids were unaware of the number of STDs in existence and the symptoms. A few of my students were homosexual, and others were heterosexual but needed to learn the facts quickly. Their behavior of engaging in sexual activities with multiple partners puts them at risk for contracting and giving STDs.

During our sessions, we discussed whatever problems were troubling them. But often, the topic returned to relationships, past and present. As their case manager, I did my best to develop goals and a plan. I informed them of STDs, especially HIV/AIDS and Herpes, which don't have a cure. Showing them pictures of physical symptoms, telling them statistics of adolescents with certain STDs, distributing information on free test sites, and sharing my experience working with HIV/AIDS positive young men didn't seem to make a difference in some. They continued to engage in risky behavior.

To add insult to injury, many didn't have support from their parents. They wouldn't accept having a gay son primarily because of their religious and cultural beliefs. Others didn't see eye-to-eye with their parents on anything. I believe their lack of an emotional attachment to mom or dad increased thirst for sexual activity.

While I tried my best to remain impartial and not attached to my teens, there are several I still worry about now that I'm no longer working at the Teen Center. It was apparent they struggled with mental health issues, but their parents refused to allow sessions with our mental health clinician. In New Jersey, a child 16 and older can receive mental health services from a licensed professional without a parent or guardian's consent (5). Although the Keystone Law is helping more adolescents than before its creation, students like my previous clients remain in need until their 16th birthday.

## Five Tips for STD Prevention

Sexually transmitted diseases might go away with the assistance of medication. Some STDs require a prescription to reduce the symptoms, while other STDs could lead to your death. If you're concerned, your teen might be sexually active, sit down and talk with them. Let them know their options for prevention.

Please review the list below, which offers ideas on how to keep teens safe.

1. Use latex condoms every time you have sex
2. Don't have multiple sex partners
3. Get tested routinely for STDs
4. Find out if or when your partner got tested
5. Abstain from sexual activity

Although this list isn't comprehensive, it covers actions to prevent the contraction of STDs. For more ways to stay safe, check out WebMD, and other reputable health sites.

## Stay Informed

STDs are a part of engaging in adult activities. No parent wants their child to contract a disease, especially a preventable one. To open the dialogue of prevention, use the information presented, and please continue to research.

## Discussion Questions

1. Have you or someone you know contracted an STD? If so, was it treatable with medications?

2. Do you think adolescents take STDs seriously? Why? Why not?

3. Do you practice safe sex? Why? Why not?

# Chapter Four

# What You Need to Know About Pregnancy Prevention

Teen pregnancy is a concern for each generation because of the impact it causes. Each case of pregnancy is unique and should be handled accordingly by the adolescents and their parents. However, there are some actions to enforce before conception occurs.

## What Can Be Done to Prevent Teen Pregnancy?

The days of locking your daughter away until you select a husband don't exist anymore, at least not in most developing countries such as the U.S. and Canada. Forcing a girl to wear a chastity belt will land you in jail. So what are concerned parents and caregivers to do in the quest for pregnancy prevention success?

When handling a complicated issue like teen pregnancy, there are numerous ways to implement a prevention strategy. But parents shouldn't feel like they are alone in this process. If your teen is fortunate enough to have a teen center in their school, please utilize it. Concerned parents contacted the staff with questions and requests regularly. Not all requests were fulfilled through the Teen Center, but we tried to link parents to the right people.

## Teen Center

Our Teen Center had a staff of four, including the program director, mental health clinician, a full-time and a part-time case manager. We also received the help of interns from the local university. I shared an office with the other case manager, and the mental health clinician had an office too. All of us were able to speak with students about teen pregnancy, but the case managers typically handled it since it fell under social services.

However, if the student exemplified mental health issues such as depression or anxiety because of the situation, they could begin therapy after the intake packet completion. The steps of pregnancy prevention consisted of bulletin boards, table events, one-on-one sessions, educational videos, and the Baby Think It Over group.

## Bulletin Board

The bulletin board gave tips on pregnancy prevention. It also showed the disadvantages of becoming an adolescent parent.

## Table Events

Table events got us out of the Teen Center and into the faces of more students. It opened the door to dialogue and new people signing up.

## Educational Shows

During the freshman summer program, an episode *of Degrassi, the Next Generation,* which showed an unexpected pregnancy, captivated them. Although the majority of the kids wanted to watch more episodes, no more were shown. The topic triggered memories of a participant's life as the daughter of a teen mom. While it wasn't my intention to upset anyone, I understand why using caution was necessary. Therefore, episodes of teen pregnancy aired during the pregnancy prevention group.

## One-On-One Sessions

As previously stated, life at the Teen Center rarely slowed down. We received referrals and drop-ins daily. My clients confided in me if something happened to them. One of my regulars came to see me because of a pregnancy scare with his girlfriend. He wasn't his usual upbeat self, so I knew something was up. He told me that his girlfriend's period was late and asked what she could do. I asked if the girl would consider coming to speak with me, but he said no.

I told him where he could purchase a pregnancy test and her options if she were pregnant. The pamphlets included were for local free clinics, Planned Parenthood locations, and birth control options. With a heavy heart, I expressed my relief that he came to discuss it and asked him to update me after the test.

A day or two later, he returned to say she wasn't pregnant. I congratulated him and discussed the importance of using condoms because pregnancy isn't the only unwanted result of unprotected sex.

## <u>Baby Think It Over</u>

Meeting with teens one-on-one is time-consuming if your goal is to inform a more sizable number. Another way the Teen Center spread the knowledge of pregnancy prevention was with the Baby Think It Over group. The group was open to boys and girls and met once a week after-school for an average of six weeks.

The participants learned about different forms of birth control, such as abstinence and condoms. After the prevention information came the knowledge of what happens if a pregnancy occurs. The topics of pregnancy nutrition, cost of living, child abuse discussions, activities of developing a budget, and the cost of baby supplies entertained and educated the group members.

During this group, the teens disclosed the current pregnant girls in the school and voiced their opinions. Many of the girls enjoyed babysitting, but they didn't want to start a family while in high school. If their views on being a teen mother were rose-colored at the beginning of the group, that faded after taking the computerized baby doll home over the weekend.

While you try to prepare the kids in the weeks leading up to the doll distribution, nothing works like a touch of reality. I always made sure to arrive a little early on a Monday when the dolls came back because there was usually a line to return them.

The final group session allowed us to discuss their experiences caring for the dolls. We also enjoyed snacks and a video. It was an enjoyable way to end a life-changing group.

Unfortunately, not all of the group members lasted the entire six weeks. One student came to the first meeting but didn't return. Several months later, she visited the Teen Center with the news of expecting her first child. We talked, and she admitted regret in not finishing the group. While there's no guarantee the group would have changed her unexpected pregnancy status, it could have given her information necessary for an expectant mother.

## Parents

When it comes to parents handling pregnancy prevention, there is no superior process. However, some actions might produce more successful results. If you're a parent of a teen attending a school with a Teen Center, please encourage them to take advantage of their services. It may lessen some of the things you need to do. Plus, teens sometimes feel more comfortable talking with an adult that isn't their parent.

But it's still important for parents and caregivers to approach this topic right before, during, and after middle school. 3.9 percent of teens younger than 13 (6) engaged in their first sexual activity. Although this percentage is low, it's still alarming. Therefore, you should review the tips below for how to manage pregnancy prevention with your adolescent.

- Sit down and discuss sex, contraception, and
- STD's
- Schedule a Gynecologist appointment for your sexually active daughter
- If your son or daughter is sexually active, get them

- tested for STD's
- Decide the right type of birth control for your teens
- Educate your teens on what life is like for teen parents
- Let your son or daughter know both are responsible when a baby is conceived
- Ensure they know abstinence is the most effective method of pregnancy and STD prevention
- Be careful of parentification and allowing your teen to raise their siblings

While you might believe discussing this subject up with your kid before middle school is too young, you don't want them to learn the wrong information from peers. As a parent, you want to protect your kids even if you can't be present 24/7. So, start laying the foundation for an empowered teen aware of the facts and resources available.

## Discussion Questions

1.  Have you or someone you know experienced a teen pregnancy?

2.  How was the situation handled?

3.  What would you do if your teen son or daughter were expecting a child?

4.  How old was your son or daughter when you began pregnancy prevention discussions?

# Chapter Five

# **Adolescents and Child Abuse**

---

A fter tossing and turning all night only to stare at the clock and read "5:50," you have two options. You either lie in bed until 7:15 or get up and drag around the house. Neither option sounds pleasing, but getting out of bed without a restful night of sleep was typical.

The problem was quieting my mind. It seemed impossible with so many things to do and the constant threat of removing a child from their home. Sometimes you'd get lucky, and your body would fall into slumber out of sheer exhaustion. But after a while, your body moves past the exhaustion and runs on autopilot.

The dreaded car ride to the office tangled my stomach in knots. The anxiety of another upset client calling my extension hovered over my head. Yet most of all, my job at D.C.P.P. revolved around child abuse and neglect. Therefore, I chose to leave for a less insane position.

Fast forward to my time at the teen center, and you'd think those days of seeing abused or neglected kids had ended. Unfortunately, you see abuse and neglected kids doing any job that deals with the public or large groups of students. Working in a school-based youth program was no exception.

## What is Child Abuse and Neglect?

The Department of Children and Families of New Jersey defines child abuse as emotional, physical, or sexual harm or risk of injury to a child below 18. The perpetrator is a caregiver or parent of the child or adolescent.

A child's neglect happens when a parent or caregiver doesn't give necessary basic needs such as clothing, food, shelter, medical care, education, or adequate supervision (7).

## Abused or Neglected Students

Working in child protective services taught me that abuse and neglect occur in every type of home and every income level regardless of race or gender. When students were dealing with current or healing from previous abuse or neglect and came to the Teen Center, they appeared like everyone else. You wouldn't know the painful memories lying beneath the surface unless you asked. Most of them became accustomed to going about their day and portraying a "normal" teen.

### <u>Student One</u>

Student One lived in a resource home due to the murder of both parents. The lack of a competent caregiver took a toll on Student One's self-esteem, quality of life, and grades. Resource homes should have offered Student One a chance to focus on being a teen.

However, the current resource home was not the ideal living situation it should have been. Through frequent visits to the Teen Center, we discussed Student One's new struggles in private. This adolescent now lived with an unhelpful resource parent.

Student One wanted a job but struggled to find employment because of transportation issues and eventually gave up. Whenever I asked if the caseworker was aware of the situation, Student One said the caseworker didn't do anything.

Eventually, Student One received permission to stay with a friend's family. The stressors of juggling school, work and making ends meet concluded. Living in a stable home allowed the adolescent the opportunity to relax and have fun.

By utilizing the Teen Center for counseling, linkage to outside resources, college tours, help with applications, and a safe place to visit, Student One overcame many obstacles. The tears in my eyes flowed when I heard the student's name called to come to get the diploma. I knew the struggles weren't over, but new doors opened through college acceptance.

## Student Two

Student Two's abuse occurred prior to the beginning of middle school. Although the student opened up about what happened, the teen denied needing therapy with our mental health clinician.

The referral I received about the student made it seem as though the death of the grandmother and moving into a new house created anxiety. Yet, the student excelled in school and extracurricular activities. In a situation like this, you can't force someone to enter into mental health services. But I did extend invitations to Teen Center events and did regular check-ins to ensure nothing serious needed discussion.

## Student Three

When it comes to memorable students, they'll always stay with you. Student Three blew into my life like a tornado. Filled with energy and blessed with a warm smile, this student embodied a fighter's spirit disguised as a typical teen. Yet the personal life of this Teen Center attendee was anything but ordinary.

Tragedy struck this student's life through the unexpected loss of a home by a fire and a sibling's death. The timing is never right to face such emotional devastation.

Conversing with this intelligent, yet quick-tempered teen, Ilearned of a sometimes-chaotic home and past allegations of abuse. Although no injuries occurred during the period in which our sessions occurred, Student Three enjoyed talking to lessen the sting of losing a close loved one. Plus, the Teen Center's support provided a haven while the student awaited grief counseling.

After departing the Teen Center, I often think of Student Three and all the others, which allowed me to help them, even if it was by listening or getting the printer to work.

## Student Four

Student Four needed the Division of Child Protection and Permanency (D.C.P.P.) called. The allegations involved abuse and neglect by the grandparents. The close friend that heard of the abuse accompanied the student to my office. My mind raced while trying to focus. During the call to the D.C.P.P. hotline, I watched as the student's face appeared worried. Student Four's friend disclosed how

Student Four revealed the information. The hotline worker scheduled an appointment at the school within two hours.

After the call, the friend returned to class, and my conversation with Student Four began. I reassured the adolescent that whatever may or may not have happened was the responsibility of the grandparents.

The discussion was brief. Eventually, the caseworker arrived and asked to borrow my office for the interview. I waited out in the common area during the conversation. It ended with both the caseworker and student leaving together for the main office.

The next day, I followed up with my student and heard about how the evening went. As expected, the grandparents were upset over the situation but ensured Student Four knew of their love. But again, I reassured the adolescent that it was the right thing to report what happened.

From that day on, I met with Student Four to discuss the aftermath of the D.C.P.P. case and its subsequent closing due to unfounded allegations.

Student Four continued to focus on school, hobbies and attending family counseling with the grandparents.

## Child Abuse Prevention Tips for Parents

Prevention is essential to most unpleasant issues, and child abuse is no exception. Child abuse and neglect are preventable, but often parents or caregivers don't know how to prepare for the possibility. While the list below isn't comprehensive, it provides an overview of ways to keep you and your teen safe.

- Wait until you're ready to have kids
- Get help for addiction issues
- Take parenting courses and read books
- Join a parenting support group
- Save money before starting a family
- Ask for assistance
- Be cautious of babysitters and the people around your kids
- Give relief to another parent who needs it
- Increase your family's income
- Give yourself regular breaks from the kids

- Allow your parenting style to evolve as your child ages
- Seek counseling if necessary

## How Did the Teen Center Promote Prevention?

The Teen Center offered students the opportunity to speak with professionals who could listen and link them to the right resources. Table events and discussions helped to promote child abuse prevention. Placing ourselves within the cafeteria gave students the ability to speak to us. Although students could access our services whenever needed, sometimes scheduling conflicts created difficulty getting out of class.

Opening up about my previous position of working at D.C.P.P. enabled kids to ask me questions related explicitly to abuse or neglect. I received a lot of "what if" scenario questions, but it made me feel good to help them. Too many teens go through life, feeling unwanted and misunderstood. It's nice for them to have a place to escape the noise of the hallway and classrooms.

If time permitted, we'd also discuss a favorite TV show of ours, *Law and Order: SVU*. I've never missed an episode, and many of our participants saw themselves in the characters onscreen. They also admired the role of Captain Olivia Benson played flawlessly by Mariska Hargitay. What's not to love? Both on and off-screen, Mariska advocates for child abuse, domestic violence, and sexual assault. Because her actions are genuine, the teens and I continue coming back season after season.

## Discussion Questions

1. Have you or someone you know experienced child abuse?

2. If so, was it ever reported? What was the outcome?

3. Would you feel comfortable speaking up if you were being abused? Why? Why not?

# Part III

# Mental Health Matters

# Chapter Six

# Teen Mental Health Awareness

——◈◈◈◈◈——

**B**eing a teen in the 1990s allowed me to grow up without social media, cyberbullying, and cell phones in every classroom. Sure, cell phones and the internet existed, but it hadn't reached the technological advancements yet to come.

Adolescents now have the blessing and burden of being connected to their friends or enemies day and night. They complete school assignments online and write essays on tablets. But the presence of electronic devices also takes away from being in the moment. Adolescent exposure to inappropriate material, negative comments about themselves on social media or in text messages, and playing video games late at night impact their quality of life.

Adolescence is tough enough without the added issue of cyberattacks, lack of sleep, and living in a fantasy reality. Not all teens have difficulty with these issues, but these are some problems parents and caregivers could prevent. Ensuring teens thrive during their transition from a child into a young adult is essential. While there isn't a magic formula for preventing mental health issues, some actions could lead to positive results.

## What is Mental Health?

Mental health is a combination of "emotional, psychological, and social well-being (8)." Mental health impacts the actions, feelings, and thoughts of a person. It allows us to function in our day-to-day lives. When issues arise, a person might struggle to get out of bed, practice hygiene, attend school, work, and maintain relationships. Therefore, it's critical to take care of yourself, learn warning signs of distress, and seek help when necessary.

## Mental Health Illness

Mental illness is a disorder that impacts a person's ability to function (9). Depending on the condition, feeling, thinking, behavior or mood might change.

My job as a case manager required me to screen students during sessions to determine whether a referral to our mental health clinician was necessary. During my time at the Teen Center, anxiety and depression required the most referrals from me.

## Anxiety

Children and adolescents struggling with "the fears and worries" of anxiety might have difficulty in school, in the home, or engaging with peers (10). Although symptoms vary, a teen might experience rapid heartbeat, sweating, headaches, fatigue, difficulty breathing, and stomachaches. These symptoms might develop due to upcoming exams, sporting events, speaking with a crush, public speaking, or disruptive home.

## Depression

The lingering feeling of sadness or helplessness might result in a depression diagnosis. Symptoms of depression include irritability, hopelessness, difficulty sleeping or increased sleeping, unable to concentrate, loss of enjoyment in activities, poor hygiene, or isolation. The causes of depression include the death of a loved one, discord in the home, divorce, separation from a parent, bullying, or gender identity issues.

Gender identity disorder can cause a person to feel alone or ashamed because of the fear of rejection from family and friends if they decide to change their outer appearance to align with the gender that represents how they feel inside (11). If their friends or peers aren't empathetic to transgender people, then teens with gender identity issues are at risk for developing depression. Just like all adolescents, they need to know someone supports them no matter which gender feels right. If the depression progresses, the teen might be in danger of developing suicidal ideations or self-harming.

## What is Mental Health Awareness?

Mental health awareness involves removing the stigma of mental health issues through advocacy, discussions, events, media coverage, and screenings.

In the U.S., we celebrate Mental Health Awareness Week during the first full week in October. Mental Health Awareness Month is celebrated in May. National Children's Mental Health Awareness Day is on the Thursday of the first full week in May and focuses on a specific topic such as suicide or depression.

## How Did the Teen Center Boost Awareness?

The Teen Center takes mental health issues and awareness seriously. Since the program and services are available year-round, watching for symptoms and raising awareness happened daily. The school-based youth services programs were ahead of changing legislature in the state of New Jersey.

Starting in August 2019, Senate Bill 2861 requires public schools must include mental health into the health class curriculum for students in grades K-12 (12). S2861 is an impressive achievement and a step in the right direction.

But Teen Centers have the advantage of raising awareness about mental health each day.

## Table Events

Utilizing table events in the cafeteria allowed us to be seen by more students than usual. We also set up a table during Back to School Night, the Activities Carnival, and Freshman Orientation.

## Messages of Hope

In May, we celebrated Mental Health Awareness Month and National Children's Mental Health Awareness Day through Messages of Hope. The Program Director and Mental Health Clinician coordinated the event at our high school. The local newspaper came to write a feature on the yearly activity.

The weeks leading up to the event involved asking Teen Center attendees if they would like to participate. Students received a cloth square. A statement, quote, or picture went onto the square to encourage other children and adolescents dealing with mental health issues.

The squares were made into a quilt and hung inside the common area. On the day of Messages of Hope, the teen center staff, students, and press members walked to the front of the school. Students used colored chalk to write a message of hope for mental health awareness.

Afterward, the kids who missed their lunch periods ate pizza. It was nice to see the kids having fun and supporting each other.

## Mindfulness Instructor

The Program Director hired a mindfulness instructor with experience at another local Teen Center. The instructor would come once a week to practice deep breathing exercises and give classroom presentations. While the instructor encountered resistance from some students, many enjoyed participating in the activities.

The popularity of the mindfulness activities opened the door for more interaction between the students and the instructor. It became another outlet for the kids to decompress after an argument, lousy score on an exam, or relationship issues.

## Parental Tips for Mental Health Awareness

Some parents are fortunate to have a mental health or social service background or personal experience. But many others don't have that luxury. If you're a parent unfamiliar with mental health, it's wise to learn the signs of anxiety, depression, and other disorders. Learning the signs could ensure your teen doesn't fall through the cracks.

Reading articles and books on teen mental health disorders will help you develop a better understanding of what your kid is feeling. Gaining knowledge also empowers you to give the right type of assistance.

Listening to what your son or daughter says is beneficial, too. Often, teens feel ignored and misunderstood by peers and adults. Strengthening your parent/child relationship lets your adolescent know they have support.

If you suspect your kid struggles with a mental health issue, talk with them, speak to their school social worker or guidance counselor. Please make an appointment to get them screened by a therapist. If your teen's school has a

Teen Center, please contact them for further information on services. It's never too early or too late to get help.

## Discussion Questions

1. Is your mental health concerning for you? Why? Why not?

2. What are the available mental health resources in your school?

3. Have you ever needed to speak to someone but couldn't find a listener? How did that make you feel? What did you do instead?

# Chapter Seven

# **Grief**

---

W hether I was manning the front desk in the common area or sitting in my office, I couldn't escape the door's constant banging. That loud sound signaled the entrance of a student in need. It could be a group of tray-carrying kids looking for a table during lunch. It might be someone wanting to use the computer for a project. But the worse sights to behold were falling tears, balled up tissues, and sad eyes.

All too often, heartbreak entered the Teen Center, and it didn't care about race, gender, or wealth. The loss of a loved one strikes the soul and never leaves after its arrival. It's up to you to go through the emotions and set out to heal. That's where our involvement began.

# What is Grief?

Grief is emotional and physical pain caused by a loved one's death or the ending of a relationship. However, grief has behavioral, cognitive, cultural, spiritual, and social aspects too.

Everyone handles grief differently. There's no timeline for it because it never truly ends. While a person learns to live without someone, the pain of the separation can resurface at any time.

# Student Five

Student Five tapped my shoulder. We'd spoken out in the common area. You know, exchanging the usual "hellos." This time Student Five caught me in the cafeteria towards the end of the period.

I began the conversation with the typical "Is there anything going on? How are your classes? Is there anything you need?" ice breakers.

Student Five surprised me with, "Is it okay if I still feel sad about losing my twin brother?" My heart tinged with pain. The first anniversary of my mom's unexpected passing drew near, and it weighed heavily on my mind.

"Of course, it's okay if you feel sad. You don't ever get over losing someone, especially your twin," I offered.

The bell rang, and crowds of tray carriers and trash throwers filled the area.

"Let's sit down. I'll send your teacher an email explaining your lateness."

We found seats at a semi-clean table.

Student Five replied, "That's what I thought, but my family tells me it's time I get over it."

The anger ignited with fury. "How dare they say that to this child? Do they understand what it's like to go through this type of loss?" I wondered.

"I mean it happened three years ago, but I still miss him," Student Five said while looking down to the floor.

"Listen, I understand some people believe they are helping by saying some things. But you shouldn't feel guilty about your sadness. I lost my mom last year, and I miss her every day. I don't think I'll ever stop missing her," I replied.

Student Five's face relaxed and responded with, "I'm sorry to hear about your mom."

"Thank you. But don't allow other people's opinions to make you feel bad. I'm sure your family thinks they're doing the right thing. If you haven't experienced this type of loss, especially at a young age, you can't relate. Even my loss is different than yours," I said.

"So how do you cope with your mom's loss?" Student Five inquired.

"Well, what works for me might not work for you. But you can try grief counseling, writing, listening to music, deep breathing exercises, going out with friends, and allowing yourself to feel sad," I disclosed.

"Yeah, I like listening to music and going out. I'll try the breathing too," Student Five replied.

"Well, if you're feeling better do you want to return to

class," I stated.

"Yeah, that's cool," said Student Five.

"Okay. I'll check in with you next week to see how you're doing, but if you need to talk, just come and see me," I told the teen.

The next day I looked for Student Five at lunch to make sure nothing else occurred. But Student Five was absent. When I looked up the kid's profile in Genesis, the profile's status read "withdrawn."

My heart sank. I never saw Student Five again, but I got closure through the friends left behind that the kid was doing okay.

## School-Wide Grieving

A 1980s lite rock song played as the morning came into focus. Although my departure from the Teen Center lay a month away, my body was in work-from-home mode. I turned on the cell phone, waiting to see if there were any messages from my co-workers or boss. To my surprise, a voicemail from the school popped up on the screen.

"Hmm, it's April, so no snowstorm closing." Just as I pressed play, more buzzing occurred to alert me to new texts. Naturally, I went into panic mode because early morning group texts never bode well for an adolescent case manager.

The voicemail alerted the school staff of a student's death the previous evening. Right away, I needed to know who we lost. I clicked on my school email and read the shocking details. A senior died in a collision seven weeks before graduation. Although the deceased wasn't a regular attendee at the Teen Center, friends and acquaintances always visited.

I sped up the pace of dressing, feeding the cats, and heading out the door. I checked the group texts and saw they came through last night. I wished my phone hadn't been turned off early in the evening, because receiving lousy news at 6:00 AM isn't enjoyable.

A haze of shock made the minutes flow like a dream. It triggered memories of awaking to messages of my mom's hospitalization, which led to her unexpected death. While my mind tried to function, it reminded me that I'd made the right decision to leave case management.

We all arrived to weather the storm together. Each workday always followed its unexpected course, but anything could happen when something out of the ordinary occurred.

The day progressed with the slamming door, eerie quietness, and feeling lost. Those closest to the teen opted to miss school. But my heart broke when our mental health clinician told me many of our participants knew the deceased.

I prepared by reviewing articles on grief and reviewing my continuing journey of healing.

Everyone at the Teen Center and within the school shared the loss of the young soul. But I knew grieving kids would eventually visit and chat.

My gaze poured over the information on the computer screen as the new groups of kids trickled inside. I closed the articles and prepared to listen to the confusion, heartbreak, and questioning of youth.

Over the days and weeks after the death, memorials

happened. Teachers and Guidance Counselors held their own as we all worked together to ride the wave of sadness and prepare for solemn graduation.

## Tips for Coping with Grief

People handle adverse events differently. But whether you choose to address the grief immediately or years later is up to you. There aren't magical steps to take to make the pain go away. All you can do is what works for you.

Below you'll find suggestions for ways to cope with grief.

- Counseling
- Crying
- Journaling
- Listening to music
- Resting
- Spending time outdoors
- Talking with family or friends
- Watching a funny movie

If you find your teen struggling with the loss of a close friend or family member, reach out to them. Even if your adolescent wants to be alone, it's essential to stay close and contact a grief counselor. You don't want their symptoms to escalate to self-harming activities or suicidal thoughts. But sometimes knowing someone is available to listen lessens the weight of mourning.

## Discussion Questions

1. Have you ever lost a friend or family member?
2. How did it make you feel?
3. Did you go to grief counseling? Why? Why not?

# Chapter Eight

# Bullying and What You Can Do About It

━━━━◆◇◆◇◆━━━━

**E**very year, millions of people tune in to watch Ralph Parker go head-to-head with the yellow-toothed, coonskin cap-wearing bully Scut Farkus. Although *A Christmas Story* marathon on TNT marks the end of the countdown to Christmas, it also turns a severe problem into entertainment.

Ralphie, his younger brother Randy, and two best friends live in fear of the almost daily torments by Scut and his toady Grover Gill. But once the abuse and anxiety overwhelm him, Ralphie blacks out and resorts to violence. He isn't able to stop hitting, cursing, and shaking his target until his mother intervenes, leaving Scut drenched from a bloody nose. Afterward, Ralphie realizes what's happened, and the tears fall.

Zach Ward, the actor portraying Scut, spoke out against bullying because of his personal bullying experiences and his role in *A Christmas Story.*

Many of us who grew up watching this movie find this scene hilarious, but it's also realistic. People repeatedly harassed by someone, suffer internally, and prolonged bullying might lead to dire consequences.

## What Is Bullying?

Bullying is repeated, aggressive behavior among children, adolescents, and sometimes adults (13). The bully uses their power of physical strength, popularity, or access to sensitive information to inflict harm or control.

Bullying includes name-calling, teasing, threats, spreading rumors, public embarrassment,
stealing personal items, pushing, hitting, or making inappropriate gestures. Bullying doesn't only  occur in school. It might happen in the mall, on the bus, at sports events, or through texts and social media. But regardless of the location of an attack, bullying isn't right and should be stopped.

# What the Teen Center Did To Handle Bullying

As students returned to classes in September, the part-time case manager and I scheduled our Bullying and Teen Dating Violence presentations. Depending on the teacher's availability, we made the rounds of Health classes.

After completing the presentations, we received questions and interested newcomers to the Teen Center. Many of the kids experienced bullying or knew people who did. The hesitation in some people raising their hands and looking around the room before speaking confirmed what most adolescents know. You don't snitch on a bully because it could make things worse. However, we made it clear that not reporting or intervening is the same as bullying someone yourself. This information was reiterated when a bullying incident was filmed off school grounds and circulated. While it was reported to the administration, it could have been handled better by the adolescent witnesses.

Bullying incidents are why presentations and one-on-one sessions are necessary because they remove the stigma of asking for help. Whenever asked, we accompanied students to the Principal's office because of fear their bully might retaliate in the halls, bathroom, or bus ride home. Sitting beside a student disclosing their bullying ordeal showed the administration we cared about the pupils and expected them to be proactive like us.

## Student Six

While working with the public, colorful characters found their way to me. As a case manager in a high school Teen Center, I observed the typical awkward behavior of kids finding themselves and trying to survive. But nothing could have prepared me for Student Six.

Student Six came into my life with a fixed smile and boisterous personality.

Our first session initially dragged as the teen sat directly across from me, fidgeting and silently smirking. My attempts to break the ice crashed.

Yet the teen's fondness for humming opened up the conversation, which led to discussing Student Six's love for singing.

Soon our discussions grew more involved when I'd hear comments like, "I punched a guy in my class. Look at my knuckles." I'd ask whether a doctor saw the swollen hands and developed a plan to address anger issues.

As soon as that issue got contained, we'd deal with "B* started talking shit about me. So I said I'd beat his ass the next time he says something." Then we'd move on to ignoring instigators who like getting a reaction.

Although all allegations of bullying were reported to teachers and the principal, Student Six enjoyed fighting.

Things took a turn as stories became more outlandish, and I heard statements like, "My uncle broke my phone last night, and he threatened to kill me if I said anything." Alarmed by this revelation, a call to Student Six's father confirmed no cell phone was damaged, nor did an uncle exist.

While the adolescent had permission to come to the Teen Center to "cool down," it couldn't become an everyday, all-day thing.

I put my foot down when Student Six began missing class more often. The reasons for the absences didn't justify repeatedly visiting the Teen Center. Student Six had the skills to self-calm but didn't want to be in class unless it involved music.

We explained to Student Six that I had other clients to see. I couldn't drop everything to speak about plans to move in with a family friend that produced music in L.A. or proof of alien conspiracies.

My conversations with dad disclosed Student Six exaggerated the information to gain attention. Thankfully, Student Six continued appointments with an outside mental health provider.

By my last week at the Teen Center, I'd had a final session with Student Six. Surprisingly, the teen handled better than expected, even though speaking to someone new would take adjustment.

But I told Student Six I'd attend the graduation.

## Bullying's Impact on Teens

A teen with a bully might begin showing signs of stress. Not all victims wear their bullying on the outside. Many bullied kids feel anxiety, depression, loneliness, and sadness, but their appearance doesn't match their emotions.

Below is a list of what to look for when someone gets bullied (14).

- Headaches, stomach aches, illness or pretending to be sick
- Nightmares or insomnia
- Low self-esteem
- Isolation from friends
- Loss of interest in hobbies, social gatherings
- Hunger due to skipping lunch or lack of appetite
- Missing or damaged items
- Injuries
- Poor G.P.A. or skipping school
- Self-harming, running away, suicidal ideations, or retaliation

## How to Spot a Bully

It's essential to know the signs of a bully and discuss them with your son or daughter for protection. Not all bullies look the same. A bully can be male or female, and any race, but bullies tend to share specific characteristics.

Bullies tend to have friends who also bully others. Bullies exhibit aggressive behavior by fighting, blaming others for personal problems, are competitive, and frequently get into trouble (14).

Because bullies might have extenuating circumstances at home, they might turn to alcohol, substance abuse, have sex at an early age, or perform criminal activities.

## Bullying Prevention Tips

Prevention happens when you take the first step towards educating and acting fast. Teens and adults sometimes miss a bullying episode. If this is the case, the situation doesn't get resolved.

Being proactive includes discussing bullying with your

teens. Ensuring they understand bullying by giving examples. Next, talking about what to do if they suspect they have a bully. This discussion might include defending themselves if no one is around, escape isn't possible, and physical harm (without a weapon) is imminent. Consider placing your teen into self-defense classes or martial arts.

Review the importance of reporting bullying to school officials. If one person doesn't help them, find someone who will like a social worker or Teen Center staff member.

Letting your teen know they are supported might decrease feelings of anxiety, depression, and loneliness.

Giving your teen the tools for self-protection is crucial. Most schools don't want students to engage in physical altercations, but there are times when defending yourself is required.

However, there is a difference between defending and attempting to harm another severely. Make sure your adolescent knows what to do.

## Discussion Questions

1. Have you ever bullied someone or been bullied?

2. What did you do to stop it?

3. Did you report it to the school staff or the police?

# Chapter Nine

# **The Pain of Suicide**

———◈———

**T**wo things helped to shape my early opinion of suicide. One of them was the 1988 movie, *Permanent Record*, starring a young Keanu Reeves. In the film, his character Chris struggles with witnessing his best-friend David die. The story progresses with Chris, the school, and the community trying to come to terms with the tragic death. Some of the faculty can't understand why Chris isn't focused or able to keep up with the school's production of the *H.M.S. Pinafore*. Even more alarming is the school forbids the pupils to mourn with a Memorial after they learn David died by suicide.

The second thing to broaden my view of suicide involved a friend I'd made during my freshman year of high school. P's* past read like an episode of *Degrassi, The Next Generation*. She was sexually active with a history of abuse.

One day, I came home to find a voicemail on my answering machine. She explained taking too many over the counter painkillers, her fondness of our friendship, and a drowsy good-bye.

I sat on my daybed with a knotted stomach and a lightheaded feeling. I called P's home but didn't get an answer. My mom wasn't a fan of our friendship, so I didn't want to tell her initially. I waited and waited and waited.

Eventually, P phoned to say the pills made her fall asleep, but she was okay.

The revelation triggered both relief and anger in me. I didn't know how to understand her pain nor the selfish act of making me one of the last people she contacted. All I knew is that things changed between us. Our friendship grew strained and eventually dissolved after she transferred schools.

But if I could redo this phase of my adolescence, I'd do a lot of things differently.

# What is Suicide?

Suicide is the intentional ending of your life. Suicide methods include ingesting poison, overdosing on medication, cutting your wrists, a gunshot wound to the head, and hanging.

While it might seem difficult to believe your pre-teen or adolescent child would consider killing themselves, the numbers speak the reality of the situation.

Suicide rates for children ages 10-14 tripled from 2007 to 2017. As of 2017, suicide is the second-highest contributor to death for people ages 10 to 24, beating out homicide, which is third (15).

# Is Suicide Preventable?

Yes, suicide prevention is possible if people learn the signs of a person contemplating and planning to end their life. However, suicide is complicated and involves varying contributing factors, so in some cases, a person might succeed in ending their life regardless of the actions taken to prevent it.

## Suicide Prevention Tips

Preventing suicide starts by learning the signs and following through on your intentions. If you want to protect your teen from suicide, here is a list of things to do.

- Communicate with your son and daughter
- Discuss the signs of suicide
- Don't dismiss disclosures of depression or suicidal
- thoughts
- Please give them the phone number to the National Suicide Prevention Lifeline
- Watch for changes in behavior and mood
- Offer counseling
- Research available mental health options in their school

## Suicide Prevention at the Teen Center

September brought much activity and preparation to the Teen Center. Unfortunately, World Suicide Prevention Day often intersected with Labor Day weekend or the first week of classes. During this time, it wasn't easy to hold events or get students down to the Teen Center because teachers needed to begin their lessons.

Therefore, our attention switched to including suicide prevention during a tabling event in the cafeteria, one-on-one discussions, displaying suicide prevention brochures, and including it during Mental Health Awareness Month.

Thankfully, our classroom visits and word-of-mouth informed kids of our ability to help them if suicidal thoughts arose.

## Handling Teens in Need

Social Work comes with ethics, protocol, and confidentiality. All of these topics received equal attention at the Teen Center. Whenever faced with a student who was harboring self-harming thoughts or a suicide plan, specific steps were taken to ensure safety.

When a student disclosed suicidal thoughts, my ears perked up. I had to ask questions to decipher if the teen currently felt like dying by suicide or felt that way recently. In the situation of a student wanting to end their life at that moment, one of two things would occur. If the student were already a mental health client, then our mental health clinician would take over and begin screening. During the screening, the local psychiatric intervention program would get contacted for the student intake.

If the student wasn't a mental health client, the school would be contacted and takeover the necessary steps. It was always essential to stay with the student after the disclosure of suicidal thoughts. But during my first two cases, my anxiety kicked in, and I briefly left my office to ask questions and look for my boss. I took responsibility for the mistake, but the fear of messing up never left me.

During my time at D.C.P.P., I always feared to have to do a home removal. Working at the Teen Center brought the fear that one of my kids would commit suicide, and no one wants that pain. But thankfully, no one on my caseload took their own life.

## Timing Counts

None of us is guaranteed another day. If your teen is considering suicide, please act now. When immediate help is necessary, please call the police. The Mental Illness

Policy organization recommends choosing your words carefully when calling 9-1-1 (16). The organization suggests telling dispatchers there is an emotionally disturbed person or EDP acting "violent or suicidal."

Showing the dispatcher you know the person is planning to "die by hanging or slit his wrists" because of a note you found or a statement made might compel the police to intervene. But depending on your location, they might transfer you to a crisis worker to get an emergency evaluation.

If your teen needs to talk to someone, offer your ears, or give them the National Suicide Prevention Lifeline phone number. Mention the website You Matter.suicidepreventionlifeline.org since it's a place for adolescents and young adults to discuss mental health and wellness stories.

To familiarize yourself and your teen with suicide information, please visit the Stop Suicide website (17). The website offers specific behaviors done and statements made by people thinking about suicide. It also describes how to react if you believe your teen is suicidal. But whether you're 25 percent or 95 percent sure the signs are there, the best thing to do is take action because ignoring the signs might result in a preventable loss of life.

## Discussion Questions

1. Have you ever thought about attempting suicide? Why? Why not?

2. Do you know anyone who died by suicide? If so, have you sought therapy to discuss it? Why? Why not?

3. Why do you think suicide rates are high for teens?

# Part IV

# Transitioning into Adulthood

# Chapter Ten

# Jobs, Colleges, and Scholarships, Oh My!

———❖———

**E**very year the frown/smile effect occurred due to employment, college searches, and the need for scholarships. A frown usually led to a smile once the issue got resolved. But the smile changed back into a frown once the reality of the situation came into view.

Searching for your first job and college are milestones for high school students. Both signal the transition from childhood to adulthood. Yet the task is tricky when factoring in the time, effort, and transportation needed to accomplish it.

Although many parents don't want their teen saddled with the responsibility of worrying about bills or the cost of living, it's a real concern for many adolescents. In the United States, the monthly cost of living is $2,638 for a single person, which translates to an annual cost of $31,656 (18). In New Jersey, a resident must earn $56,810 per year to afford a two-bedroom rental without spending more than 30 percent of their gross income (19).

When reviewing the high cost of living, it's not surprising students want to gain employment. Many teens help supplement the family income or pay for their necessities to ease their parents' burden. The need to work and the family's economic status also plays a crucial role in whether a student will apply for college.

The average cost of an in-state New Jersey college was $16,709 during the 2018-2019 school year, which is $2,302 higher than the U.S. average (20).

Since the cost of education and living pose extra stress on high school students, it's essential to provide guidance and assistance to overcome obstacles.

## How Did the Teen Center Handle Job Searches?

Job hunting in high school isn't easy anymore. I grew up listening to stories from my mom about how she started her first job at 14 with working papers. But many companies and organizations have increased the minimum working age to 16, 17, or 18, depending on the type of industry.

So what's a broke high schooler to do? Well, they'd come into the common area and ask for help. I'd go into detective mode and scour the internet for all available jobs for the adolescent population. Looking for a job wasn't a walk in the park because many kids couldn't rely on their parents for a ride. Therefore, the teen needed access to public transportation, which wasn't a simple feat for our rural students.

After getting flooded with questions, I decided to create a list of local hiring businesses. I also compiled a list of companies willing to accept 15 and 16-year-olds. Some employed kids would bring in flyers if their company needed workers. Many kids relied on the declining mall and McDonald's for employment. McDonald's employees ranted about customers ordering hundreds of cheeseburgers in the drive-thru or requesting unassembled burgers. But their battle stories didn't deter the younger kids who just needed a gig and paycheck.

If an 18-year-old had transportation, the casinos were an option, but it would require a lengthy commute by bus. But putting the advertisements in front of them wasn't enough. I'd sit down with them, help answer confusing questions in the job application, and proofread resumes. I encouraged them to always follow up with managers because it will increase their chance of an interview.

The students returned with updates as to whether they got an interview. We'd discuss how to crush it by watching videos of interview fails.

The Teen Center staff wished students good luck on their interviews and asked for updates on start dates. If a kid didn't get hired, we'd continue the job search and offer a pep talk.

Eventually, the smile of success appeared as they prepared for their first day and training. Yet the smile turned upside after the teens realized having a job meant you worked.

## How Did the Teen Center Assist in College and Scholarship Searches?

Some of my favorite one-on-one sessions included speaking with kids about their life goals. I felt fortunate to help them narrow down the selection of majors, colleges, and future careers.

If a student struggled with planning a life outside of high school, we'd discuss current hobbies and interests. I'd ask about which classes they enjoyed in school and whether they intended to go to college or a trade school after graduation.

Some students aspired to become lawyers, doctors, and writers. Others wanted to learn a trade and become an entrepreneur. Then there were students destined to join the military for the benefits of seeing the world while receiving an education.

For the students who wanted the college experience, we arranged for a tour of Rowan University. Opening teens' eyes that rarely left their county gave us joy because we knew they needed exposure to what life could be. But local colleges weren't the only institutions our kids visited.

We also promoted bus trips to Historically Black Colleges and Universities and helped cover the registration fee of those needing financial assistance.

Completing FAFSA applications, looking for scholarships, and explaining college admission applications became a habit. We all assisted students with their paperwork during our turn as coverage or one-on-one sessions. We were available to proofread application essays.

But I felt lit up inside when one of my regular visitors asked for a letter of recommendation to my alma mater. The words flowed from a genuine place and led to acceptance to the university.

While lots of our kids graduated still undecided about a future career, at least their diploma would enable them to get a job until their life paths developed.

# Tips for Parents

It might seem like common sense to many parents that your teens need help, but plenty of teens go-at-it alone. Teen Centers fill the gap for students lacking parental assistance at home that others receive. But if you want to step it up, please review the tips below for helping your kids secure employment and apply for college.

- Lead by example through working and talking about your job
- Help your teen search for jobs online and in-person
- Teach them to complete applications, resumes, and cover letters
- Review how to interview with an employer through role-playing
- Schedule college tours
- Offer to help them practice for the SATs
- Contact organizations you belong to for information on scholarships
- Start a savings account for college or post-high school life

- Find a mentor, possibly a college student, to educate your teen on their experience
- Contact your teen's Guidance Counselor or Teen Center for information on college-related activities and events

## Life after High School

It doesn't matter if you're 50 or 25; adults know the struggles attached to adulthood. Not all teens are blessed with an ideal upbringing and could use support. Asking for help doesn't make you weak; it shows you know your limits and desire improvement of your situation.

Teen Centers thrive at offering help to students in need. But if you're a parent and think you could do more for your kid, then research, talk to your teen's school, and chat with other parents. It's never too early to get your son or daughter ready for the real world.

## Discussion Questions

1. Is anyone helping you to search for jobs, colleges, or scholarships?

2. Does your school offer resources for seeking employment, colleges, and scholarships?

# Part V

# Recreation

# Chapter Eleven

# **Fun Times at the Teen Center**

———◆———

The clanking door gave way to dry heat as my slender frame began its journey to multiple wings. I noticed couples making out, teachers chatting, and Canadian geese in the grass outside the windows. The passes held safely in my grip. My squeaky black loafers scored my quick pace.

"Good morning. Good morning," flowed from my lips.

"Hey, Miss Tamika, y'all going on a trip?" asked a familiar face.

"Yes, it's tomorrow. We're going to see the Nutcracker."

"Can I go?"

"Did you sign up and turn in a permission slip?" "Nah, but I can get it to you by tomorrow morning."

"Well, are your grades good? What about absences? Any detentions, suspensions, or cutting class?"

"I haven't missed school since I was sick last month. My grades are good. I'm not failing anything. You know I don't get into trouble."

"Yeah, that's true. Okay, come get a permission slip as soon as possible. I'll double-check Genesis. If we have a spot, you can go."

"Okay, thanks. I'll come during gym."

"Alright, just make sure it's okay with your teacher." "I will. See you later.

"See ya."

Looking down at my stack of passes for the trip and today's sessions helped me find my way again. Thank goodness I had coffee and ate. It's only 7:55, and I'm already exhausted.

## Education vs. Recreation

Although our Teen Center wasn't new, it evolved to stay current with the culture and crises. Sure, we were an educational component to the school. But no teen wants to hang in a carbon copy of a classroom. Hence, walking the line between recreation and education was essential.

## Education

Before I arrived at the Teen Center, it developed a reputation for more play than work. So when shifts in management and changes to the daily schedule occurred, some attendees weren't happy. Cutting down on the use of YouTube and Netflix did reduce the amount of noise. Plus, students needing to work on assignments or study found refuge with us.

However, it also, at times, left a flat-lining feeling to the atmosphere.

Restoring balance through informative videos, discussions, guest speakers, group meetings, and mindfulness exercises ushered in the transition.

## Informative Videos

The Teen Center showed a variety of educational videos, including 20-minute shorts on specific topics like teen dating violence, sexually transmitted diseases, and homosexuality. Videos on teen job hunting, interviewing, moving into college dorms, and taking a job abroad also interested them.

## Discussions

Most days involved discussions in the common area. A debate could arise from a group of girls talking loudly about a relationship issue. We tried not to censor topics, but if it included sensitive information or made people uncomfortable, we'd suggest scheduling a one-on-one session or joining a relevant group.

## Guest Speakers

Attending a guest speaker presentation allowed students with questions about careers, teen dating violence, and police protection to voice their concerns. Inviting guest speakers to the Teen Center enticed current and new attendees to visit. Plus, it gave the teens a chance to meet professionals in their community.

## Group Meetings

Each year the Teen Center offered groups on relevant topics such as dating, pregnancy prevention, hygiene, self-esteem, body image, depression, and suicide. I facilitated the Baby Think It Over group and initially co-facilitated the Girls group before the intern took over. Our mental health clinician created an exciting and necessary group centered on the topics shown in the hit Netflix series *13 Reasons Why*. If I were still at the Teen Center, I'd consider developing a group about *On My Block*, another popular teen dramedy on Netflix. Both shows explore teen life, but one focuses on suburban kids and the other on adolescents living in a gang-infested city. The topics covered in both shows are relatable to teens and should be discussed to help process them.

## Mindfulness Exercises

The introduction of mindfulness added a layer of comfort to the often-stressed students of the Teen Center. The mindfulness coach brought truth, honesty, and new energy to our kids. By learning to control their breathing, body position, and thoughts, the teens can reduce anxiety, nervousness, and increase focus. Plus, the exercises increase calmness.

## Recreation

Everyone needs time to play, and we worked hard to provide a fun zone. Now some days were more rah rah rah than others, but when the laughter took over, it felt great. Our recreation methods included "arts 'n crafts," events, playing games, streaming movies, TV shows, and music videos, and field trips.

## Arts N Crafts

Whether a student craved decompression of their anger or anxiety, our art supplies gave them the stress relief needed. If an event or holiday drew near, we enlisted kids' help for banners, bulletin board letters, decorations, or signs. Markers, watercolors, acrylic paints, glitter glue, paint by numbers kits, construction paper, and coloring book pages provided the outlet for artistic expression.

## Events

Hosting an event at the Teen Center took collaboration and concentration to pull it off. Ensuring enough time between the concept and the actual engagement gave room for things to go amiss. Every event turned into a learning experience. Annual events included a pumpkin decorating contest for Breast Cancer Awareness Month, Thanksgiving-themed art projects and food donation, volunteering at the local food bank, Crafts N Cocoa during the holiday season, and a celebration or distribution of gifts for the graduating seniors.

## Playing Games

Unlocking the cabinets happened during the morning routine. The kids had their choice of classics like Monopoly, Jenga, Battleship, and Connect Four. But the Game of Life, Uno and Sorry were top picks for the students and me.

You never knew when things would get heated during a round of Uno, the Game of Life, or Sorry. The tricky part of playing the Game of Life was finishing. Sometimes we left the board in the corner until the players returned during study hall or lunch. When a student had a substitute, it allowed more game time due to a lack of new lessons. On Fridays, we took the Xbox out. Madden NFL and NBA 2K received the most attention. But regardless of the day, the teens could participate in a friendly competition.

## Streaming Movies, TV Shows, and Music Videos

The privilege of streaming movies, TV shows, and music videos gave the Teen Center a relaxing vibe. True, the kids weren't home, but we wanted them to unwind.

Control of the TV took adjustment for me because of my flexible nature. It didn't take long before I started putting my foot down to the kids choosing inappropriate Hip Hop or Rock songs. Many of our attendees enjoyed the 1990s and early millennium music, which triggered my high school memories.

We enjoyed game shows such as *The Price is Right, Family Feud,* and *Lingo* during the lunch periods. But everyone's go-to streaming app was Netflix. Many of the kids used personal accounts on their phones, but they requested shows like *Stranger Things* if the TV was off.

Most of the original teen-centered movies on Netflix were enjoyable. But one student made it clear that the heroine in *The Kissing Booth* was "hoing it up" by secretly dating her male BFF's brother. That comment sparked a hilarious discussion.

## Field Trips

While I loved helping teens, one of my job's best requirements was planning events and trips. Getting to attend a Teen Center field trip became the hottest ticket in school. It made people show up in droves to sign up. Random kids would trickle in for the chance to go to a Philadelphia 76ers game, *Matilda the Musical*, or the Philadelphia Zoo.

One of my favorite trips was to see the *Nutcracker* at Stockton University's Performing Arts Center (PAC). It became the first activity I organized since I began my position in early October, and no trips were taken yet.

Accompanying a group of teens to a beloved ballet excited and terrified me.

I sprang into action by calling the PAC and securing twenty-five seats, which included chaperone tickets. Next, emailing the school bus coordinator in the transportation office and scheduling a bus occurred. Then we began advertising the trip to our Teen Center participants. Many were unfamiliar with the *Nutcracker* but eager to get out of class.

Our signup sheets provided information on the date and time of departure and return. Our permission slips gave the same information, the deadline to return the form, lunch served at the Teen Center after the performance, our contact information for parents, and room for parent/guardian contact information. If an 18-year-old signed the slip, a parental signature was unnecessary. We still encouraged them to inform their parents.

The hustle and bustle of reviewing the signup sheet and checking Genesis for eligible students took time. Once a list of students existed, the creation of passes for them to leave class and come to the Teen Center was made.

Depending on the amount of time available, we either wrote out regular passes used for sessions or designed trip specific passes through an online designing website.

I tried to make my schedule light the day before a trip because there were many things to review and cross off the checklist. The day of a trip was wild cards because of students being absent, late, or turning in last-minute permission slips. Each attendee's identity needed to be on the list in Genesis and shared with the Main Office staff before departure. Sometimes this meant changing the list two or three times before walking outside and secretly thinking, "this bus better fucking be here" in my pounding head.

Noise, laughter, and excitement filled the common area as we gathered up our trip bags, list of students, and headed outside. A chatty bus ride later, we arrived with time to spare. After last-minute restroom breaks, we made two lines and awaited entrance into the theatre.

Finally, settled into our seats, my back leaned into the firm, yet comfortable cushions. I sat at the end of the row, and the other chaperones sat on the opposite side to ensure we remained a group. As the curtain rose, Tchaikovsky's enchanting melodies lulled us into the dreamland of Clara and Fritz.

"Yo! How'd that girl do that? Miss Tamika, did you see how she stood on her toes?" the Xbox enthusiast asked while watching the *Nutcracker* for the first time. Mesmerized eyes followed the dancers as they twirled and glided through the air with ease. Their years of grueling practice and obsessive dedication transferred this teen from adolescence to childhood wonder, which made the stress of coordinating and chaperoning the holiday excursion worth it.

After we returned to the Teen Center and ate, the kids expressed their thoughts about the ballet. Seeing a ballet for the first time entertained them more than anticipated even if some students fell asleep. The ladies from the dance class loved it, and the few male attendees shared their enjoyment, too.

Some trickled back into their classes to get homework or see friends who didn't go, while others remained to chat with us until dismissal.

But putting away the permission slips into everyone's charts couldn't wait until the next day even though my eyes couldn't focus on a tedious task. Pushing through was better than starting the day with yesterday's work.

During my time as a Case Manager, we'd go on to visit the Franklin Institute, the Walnut Street Theatre, the Philadelphia Zoo, and the Wildwood Boardwalk Piers. Although I didn't plan every trip, we worked together to make our ventures away from school a memorable experience.

## Discussion Questions

1. Does your school offer recreational activities, events, and trips? If so, is the admission or tickets free?

2. If your school has a Teen Center, do you participate in activities, events, or trips? Why? Why not?

3. If your school doesn't have a Teen Center, do you think it would be beneficial to open one? Why? Why not?

# Part VI

# Why Aren't There More Teen

# Centers?

# Chapter Twelve

# **The Future of Teen Centers**

S tudents and parents alike appreciated our Teen Center. Although many pupils didn't utilize the free services and join the center, plenty of them did, and it isn't difficult to understand.

Parents and guardians of Teen Center participants asked why there wasn't a center at the middle school or more high schools in the area. The short answer we'd provide is that it wasn't up to us, but the state. True, this is part of the reason for the limited number of Teen Centers throughout New Jersey. However, there is more to the story.

## Available Funding

As previously discussed, the New Jersey Department of Children and Families' (DCF) a Division of Family and Community Partnerships (FCP), and Office of School

Linked Services (OSLS) distributes the state and federal funding for a School-Based Youth Services Program (SBYSP) in a county of their choosing.

When available funds arise, a Request for Proposals (RFP) gets announced (21). The notification provides a bidder's conference date or a deadline for question submission and the due date for bid submission.

The proposal request also goes into detail about the program, the goals, the target population, the layout of the teen center, and the type of services provided. The initial review determines if the proposal meets the criteria. Acceptable proposals move on to the Proposal Evaluation Committee. The committee reviews, deliberates, and individually scores the applications.

The selected applicant must adhere to the rules and regulations in the Standard Language Document, the Contract Reimbursement Manual, and the Contract Policy and Information Manual (22). The funding is awarded after a contract negotiation, and the program must open by the agreed-upon date.

## Documentation

Where would social work be without its documentation? Documentation provides proof that something took place, and we certainly kept busy monitoring our daily activities. The program director, mental health clinician, case managers, and interns provided documentation when necessary. Whether it was daily contact notes or service reports, tracking our student interactions were essential.

The students completed the state-required Resiliency Tool two or three times per year. Our mental health organization required their surveys completed a few times per year too. After a while, the participants grew tired of taking surveys. Thus, we carefully reviewed the questions, provided candy, and explained the importance of the surveys so that they wouldn't circle any answer.

## Yearly Visits

Each year, a member of the state would visit all of the Teen Centers throughout New Jersey. The weeks leading up to it meant we all reviewed our case files to ensure correct paper placement, completed forms, and missing documents. Since we never knew which charts would get audited, that pushed us to stay focused on our case files year-round.

The visit was stressful because the state worker monopolized the case manager's office because of the filing cabinets. So, having a quiet space to speak with a student was limited, especially if the mental health clinician's office was occupied.

But we always tried our best to be cordial, even though we prayed for a speedy end and quick return to our regular day.

## Community Support

The Teen Center continues to be a vital part of the community. It allows the students and parents to receive support from the unexpected and sometimes stressful life events. But it's also a haven for kids who want to escape the loud cafeteria and bond with their peers. Plus, if your teen is lucky, he or she might get to explore the Franklin Institute or view a powerful film, free of cost.

If you're interested in your community opening a School-Based Youth Services Program, contact your local board of education to see if there are plans underway. But remember the grant money comes from the Office of School Linked Services (OSLS), so contacting them with questions is another option.

## Discussion Questions

1. If you've attended or worked in a Teen Center, what are your views?
2. What ways did they help the students?
3. Did you enjoy your time there?

# Part VII

# Relevant Information

# National Resources

**Chapter 2**- National Teen Dating Violence Abuse Hotline 1-866-331-9474

**Chapter 3**- Planned Parenthood (https://www.plannedparenthood.org/)

**Chapter 4**- Planned Parenthood (https://www.plannedparenthood.org/)

**Chapter 5**- Child Help National Child Abuse Hotline  1-800-422-4453, Healthy Families America (https://www.healthyfamiliesamerica.org/),        National Sexual Assault Hotline 1-800-656-4673

**Chapter 6**- National Alliance on Mental Illness Helpline 1-800-950-6264 Monday – Friday 10:00 AM to 6:00 PM EST  or  email  info@nami.org,  Talkspace  for  Teens (https://www.talkspace.com/blog/teen-mental-health-guide/)

**Chapter 7**- National Alliance for Grieving Children (ChildrenGrieve.org)

**Chapter 8**- Crisis Text Line (Text HELLO to 741741)

**Chapter 9**- National Suicide Prevention Lifeline 1-800-273-8255

# References

## Chapter 2

1. https://nij.ojp.gov/topics/crimes/teen-dating-violence

2. https://youth.gov/federal-links/national-teen-dating- abuse-helpline

3. https://www.dosomething.org/us/facts/11-facts-about- teen-dating-violence

## Chapter 3

4. https://www.hhs.gov/ash/oah/adolescent-development/reproductive-health-and-teen-pregnancy/stds/index.html#_ftn2

5. https://youthtoday.org/2016/03/seeking-mental-health-support-teens-helped-pass-new-law-to-access-mental-health-care-without-parental-consent/#:~:text=The%20bill%2C%20which%2 0was%2 0called,health%20care%20without%20parental%2 0conse nt.

## Chapter 4

6. http://recapp.etr.org/recapp/index.cfm?fuseactio
   n=page s.StatisticsDetail&PageID=555

## Chapter 5

7. https://www.nj.gov/dcf/reporting/defining/

## Chapter 6

8. https://www.mentalhealth.gov/basics/what-is-
   mental- health

9. https://www.cdc.gov/mentalhealth/learn/index.
   htm

10. .https://www.cdc.gov/childrensmentalhealth/fea
    tures/anxiety-depression-children.html
    https://www.glaad.org/transgender/transfaq
    https://legiscan.com/NJ/text/S2861/id/181789
    2

## Chapter 7

11. https://www.stopbullying.gov/bullying/what-is-
    bullying

12. https://www.stopbullying.gov/bullying/warning-
    signs

## Chapter 8

13. https://www.cdc.gov/nchs/data/databriefs/db35
    2-h.pdf
14. https://mentalillnesspolicy.org/coping/make911r
    espond. html
15. https://stopasuicide.org/learn-to-act.php

## Chapter 9

16. https://www.expatistan.com/cost-of-
    living/country/united-states
17. https://www.nj.com/news/2017/06/a_typical_nj
    _reside_nt_needs_to_make_this_much_to_a.html
    https://www.collegecalc.org/colleges/new-
    jersey/#:~:text=College%20Costs%20in%20New
    %20Jer
    sey&text=The%20average%20annual%20in%2Ds
    tate,or
18. %20district%20to%20attend%20college.

## Chapter 12

19. https://www.state.nj.us/dcf/providers/notices/R
    FP_5.S chool.Based.Middle.School.pdf
20. https://www.nj.gov/dcf/providers/contracting/
    manuals/

www.ingramcontent.com/pod-product-compliance
Lightning Source LLC
Chambersburg PA
CBHW051025030426
42336CB00015B/2729